BOOK 01
PRA

Prayers for women, men and kids.

Prayers for any life situation. Family prayers, prayers for depression, anxiety, self-confidence, work and success and more.

Table of content:

Morning prayers............................	6
Morning offering.....................................	7
Awesome God.......................................	8
Heavenly Father.....................................	9
Holy Father in Heaven...........................	10
I am the Child of God............................	11
Prayer for inner piece............................	12
Prayer for clear mind............................	13
Thanks for the new day.........................	14
Morning prayer for protection.................	15
Morning prayer......................................	16
Prayer of thanks for the day.....................	17
Morning Prayers For Success...................	18
Prayer for prosperity.............................	20
Early Morning Prayer............................	21
Prayers for different situations................	22
Prayer for school....................................	23
Rift among friends.................................	24
Plans..	25
Prayer for the evening meal.....................	26
Prayer before devotions..........................	27
I am thankful...	28
Prayer For The Lost...............................	29
Thank you!..	30
Tomorrow..	31
Uncertainties...	32
Salt and light...	33
Rough day...	34

Prayer for anxiety and stress......................	35
Prayer for self-confidence.........................	36
Praises...	37
Strength..	38
Anticipation..	39
Inspirational prayer................................	40
Prayer for wisdom..................................	41
Prayer for hope.....................................	42
Prayer for faith and trust........................	43
Short prayer for guidance.......................	44
Short prayer for strength........................	45
Short prayer for peace............................	46
Short prayer for protection.....................	47
Prayer for safety and protection................	48
Wedding prayer.....................................	49
Wedding prayer 2..................................	50
A prayer to recharge..............................	51
A prayer for my career............................	52
A prayer for opportunity.........................	53
A prayer for contentment........................	54
A prayer for our prayer life.....................	55
A prayer for our homes...........................	56
A prayer for financial provision................	57
A prayer for safety while travelling............	58
A prayer for health................................	59
A prayer for our kids.............................	60
A prayer to stretch time.........................	61
A prayer for Christmas...........................	62
Dedication of the day.............................	63
Afternoon prayer...................................	64
Prayer at night.....................................	65

Surrender, Healing & Forgiveness Prayers... 67
Prayer of abandonment............................ 68
Prayer of surrender................................ 69
Pleading for mercy and forgiveness of sin.... 70
Help with depression............................... 71
Overcoming sinful passions....................... 72
Prayer before the crucifix 74

Common Catholic Prayers......................... 75
Apostles Creed....................................... 76
Our Father.. 77
Hail Mary... 78
Glory be... 79
Nicene Creed... 80
Prayer before meals................................ 82
Act of Contrition 83

Prayers for every day of the week.................. 84
Sunday... 85
Monday.. 86
Tuesday.. 87
Wednesday.. 88
Thursday.. 89
Friday 90
Saturday 91

Prayers for evening and night....................... 92
For the night... 93
A short evening prayer devotion................ 94

A short evening prayer devotion 2…………... 95
Prayer of a Weary Apostle ……………………. 96
Prayer at the end of the day…………………... 97
Prayer for a day lived…………………………. 98
Prayer at the end of the day 2………………… 99
Prayer for the night coming…………………... 100
A bedtime prayer……………………………… 101
Prayer for God's protection through the night………………………………………….. 102

Prayers for family………………………............ 103
A prayer for my husband…………………….. 104
A morning prayer for my wife………………. 105
Prayer for my brother………………………… 106
Prayer for my sister…………………………… 107
Prayer for daughter's health…………………. 108
Prayer for my son……………………………… 109
Prayer for married couples………………….. 110
Prayer for your children……………………… 111
Prayer for your children 2…………………….. 112
Prayer for loved ones…………………………. 114
A prayer for family…………………………… 115
A prayer for parents………………………….. 116
A prayer for family gathering………………. 117

MORNING PRAYERS

Morning Offering

O Jesus,

through the Immaculate Heart of Mary,

I offer You my prayers, works,

joys and sufferings

of this day for all the intentions

of Your Sacred Heart,

in union with the Holy Sacrifice of the Mass

throughout the world,

in reparation for my sins,

for the intentions of all my relatives and friends,

and in particular

for the intentions of the Holy Father.

Amen.

Awesome God

Awesome God
I come before you today
With one thing to say
Thank you Abba Father

For all you've given to me
For my beautiful life,
my family and my friends
Thank you for the blessings
you gave that I never deserved
For the protection your hand provides
For the forgiveness you
offer day after day

Lord, you took my sin and my shame
You took sickness and heal all my pain
You took my darkness and gave me your light

Father thank you for all you've done in my life
And for all the blessings that I cannot see

Amen!

Heavenly Father

Heavenly Father
I come before you to thank you for a new day
Thank you, Lord, for giving me life
Thank you for loving me
What would I do without you, Lord

Thank you for my home and the beautiful family you have given me
Thank you for all the things I have and for the things I don't have
I do not worry about those things, because I know that
in due time you will provide for me
I love you, father
In the name of Jesus I pray
Amen!

Holy Father in Heaven

Holy Father in Heaven
Sometimes, my body is weak and tired
Sometimes, I have a weak will and a tendency to give up easily
Sometimes, I am so tired struggling throughout my life

You know Lord, I just can't handle it all by myself
That's why, I'm here asking you to strengthen my body, spirit and soul.
Strengthen me in the inner man
Through the power of the Holy Spirit indwelling my innermost being and personality
Invigorate and strengthen my body
Strengthen my spirit that I can resist the desires of my flesh
And set a fire down in my soul that I can't contain

God, you are my strength
I'm strong in you, Oh Lord
In the power of your might
And in the precious name Of Jesus Christ.
Amen!

I am the Child of God

I am the Child of God Almighty who is filled with grace and power
And in accordance to the word of my Father
I speak strength, power and vigor in every area of my life

I now receive strength
I receive it by faith
I drink it in

The strength of God is upon me right now
My body, mind and soul are now being restored
My strength is now being renewed

I declare that God is strengthening me and that whatever
I need to do in life: I can do it
I believe that I can do all things through the lord, my God who strengthens me
In Jesus' name
Amen!

Prayer for inner piece

Father, I feel like lost in a dessert land
Dry and thirsty for your love and strength
I'm burdened by the reality of life
And my many distressing problems

Here I am, Oh Lord
I'm longing for your grace and mercy
My soul hungers for your strength
A fresh and renewed strength
that only you can give

Lord, just speak a word and
energize my inner-being
Breathe life into my dry bones
Guide me through the maze of life
Fight my wars
And give me the peace
that surpasses all understanding
I need you
Because I can't make it on my own

In the name of Jesus, I pray

Amen!

Prayer for clear mind

Lord Jesus
I come to You now and I ask You
to wash my mind with your Blood
Cleanse out all darkness and negativity
Remove all anxiety and stress from my mind
Clear away all worries, tension and panic
I believe and declare that from this moment forward
My mind is clear and
My body is relaxed
So, Be it
Amen

Thanks for the new day

Father, I thank you for another day
I don't know what this day might bring
Therefore, I put my trust in You
Fill me with your peace
The peace that surpasses all understanding

Cover me with your presence
Comfort me in my mind
Give me fresh mental and spiritual attitude
Cause me to rest and not be stressed
Let rivers of joy and happiness
fill me every moment of this day
In the Mighty Name of Jesus, I pray
Amen

Morning prayer for protection

Father, I come before you today
To ask You to place a hedge of protection
Around me, my family, my friends, my home
my car, my properties, my pets
my workplace, my finances
And all that You have placed me in charge over

Keep me and them all from harm
Protect us on our right and on our left
Drive away darkness, danger and negativity
Cover me under your Mighty Wings
Go before me Lord and clear my path

In the Holy Name of Jesus, I Pray
Amen

Morning prayer

Father, I ask you to allow me
To dwell in your secret place
And to take refuge under your shadow
Cover me with your mighty wings

I believe and declare that
I'm shielded by your Power
I'm not afraid of darkness
I don't fear the dangers in this world
A thousand people can fall at my side
Another ten thousand at my right hand
But, nothing will happen to me

Lord, command your angels to guard me
Let them lift me up and carry me safely
Show me your salvation every single day
And allow me to enjoy the victory over evil

In the Mighty Name of Jesus
I Pray, Declare and Believe
Amen

Prayer of thanks for the day

Oh Lord, thank you for another day to live
And once again, I'm here asking for your help

I need you Almighty God
Help me with everything that I've got to do today
Also with things that will come up
that I'm not even going to know about

I ask you for grace, mercy,
guidance and protection
I ask the same for my family
and all those around me

I declare that I love you Lord
with all my heart, with all my soul,
with all my mind and with all my strength.
I love my life
I love myself
I love my family
And I love people

In Jesus' Name
Amen

Morning Prayers For Success

In the mighty name of Jesus

I pray that I will not answer to the voices of my enemies
Society will not corrupt neither my body nor my mind
My appearance will show examples of godliness
My spirit shall resist corruption
My eyes will not see indecency
My mouth shall not transgress
My hands will not do evil
And my legs shall not walk into trouble

I will not walk into adversity
because Jesus is on my side
Every misfortune will pass over

Every yoke over my life is destroyed
Every burden are now being taken away
by the power of Jesus

Any power either in the spiritual or
physical world against me shall fail
No weapon formed against me shall prosper
And every tongue that rises up in judgment will be condemned

I declare, through the authority of Jesus' name
That my mind is filled with peace

My heart is overflowed with love
My life is full of joy and happiness

I will survive this world
I will conquer
Because all things are possible
In Jesus, Amen!

Prayer for prosperity

I now accept prosperity into my life
I accept abundance into my life
I accept success and well-being

I speak into existence:
Perfect health for my body
Perfect wealth for my family
and future generations
Perfect, overwhelming and
abundant love in my life
Perfect happiness and joy in my heart
Perfect clarity and peace in my mind

I speak these things in faith
I activate them now
In the mighty name of Jesus

Victory is now flowing to me
Prosperity is mine
Success is mine

I believe so
For the earth is the Lord's my Father
and everything in it and all who live in it
Thank you, Jehovah-Jireh, my provider
Thank you for bringing
them to pass in my life
In the Name of Jesus
Amen!

Early Morning Prayer

Father in Heaven,

Thank you for watching over me as I slept through the night. Your hands of comfort and strength held me as You watched over me. Father, I love You. You love me so much and I am in awe of how amazing You truly are. As I begin my day, I simply pray that you walk with me and lead me where you please. May Your will be done this day. Amen

PRAYERS FOR DIFFERENT SITUATIONS

Prayer for School

Dear Lord,

I thank You for my school and the faculty that runs it. I pray that you will give me courage to speak the truth in the midst of lies that may be taught there. I don't ever want to accept a lie just to get a better grade. Father, be with me as I fight for truth in the midst of chaotic moments there. I know we did not evolve from monkeys because God made humans special and different from the animals. May it be that Your name be glorified today as I shine the light of Jesus Christ to a hurting world. I love You, Lord! Amen

Rifts Among Friends

Forgiving Father,

Forgive me for my own sin that is a part of the reason for a hurting friendship. I miss the way things were before our fight. Lord, I need your strength right now. I want to mend this relationship badly, but it has to be You that my friend sees in me. Father, give me the words to say today as I try to reconcile a wonderful friendship. I love You, Lord! Amen

Plans

Gracious Lord,

I have many things to do today. Bills need to be paid, a dental check-up, an oil change in my car and many other things. Father, I pray that You will be with me as I do all of these things. More importantly, I ask that You show me what plans You have prepared for me today. May it be that I don't put my plans ahead of Yours, Lord. You know what is best for me, Father, and I love You! Amen

Prayer For The Evening Meal

Father in Heaven,

Blessed be Your Name! You have brought my family back home safely through all of the things we accomplished today. I am grateful for this family You have given me. Thank you for my spouse and my children. I am truly blessed. Father, thank you for this food that has been prepared. I pray that You would use it to nourish our bodies and give us strength. Thank You most of all for Your Son, Jesus, who paid the price for our sins on the cross. Words cannot express how thankful I am for the cross. All glory, honor and praise belong to You! I love You, Father! Amen

Prayer Before Devotions

Dear Lord,

Prepare my heart for what I am about to read in Your Holy Word. I pray that You would enlighten my mind to understand everything I read. I want to know You more, Father. Show me Your will in this time as I grow closer to You through Scripture. I praise Your Holy Name, Father! I love You! Amen

I Am Thankful

Wonderful Lord,

I just want to thank You for everything You are. You have given me Jesus and now You look at me as if I am holy. I can't wrap my mind around this because I know how stained I am with sin. Father, I thank You for the beauty in nature. Thank you for lush wooded forests, crystal clear island waters, the sun for warmth and light, the moon, and the twinkling stars that You have specifically placed into constellations for us. You are wonderful and awe-inspiring, Father. I love You! Amen

Prayer For The Lost

Father, God

I pray for the lost and hurting people in this world. We are all surrounded by greed, malice, strife, conceit, pride, and many other horrible, evil things. Father, I pray that You would use me to spread Your Good News to someone today. It grieves me to know many who have died without Jesus. Hell is such a horrible place. To be eternally separated from You is hell, Father! I am eternally grateful for the cross, and Jesus' blood spilled for me. Father, I truly am in love with You! Amen

Thank You!

Dear Wonderful Father,

You have granted me another day of life to be your light on this world. Thank you for allowing me to enjoy your sunshine, my family, Your Word and Jesus today! It truly was another blessed day because You were in it, Lord. I am so thankful for all of the blessings You bestowed upon me today. I love You! Amen

Tomorrow

Father in Heaven,

If tomorrow doesn't come, I want You to know how much I love You! You have guided my steps today and brought me safely home to my family. You are truly my best friend! You sing over me daily. (Zephaniah 3:17) You rejoice over me with gladness. (Zephaniah 3:17) I am not worthy of Your affections, Father, and You don't even consider the thought of Heaven without me. Oh Lord, You really are a great God! Your love is unending and it is my portion daily! Thank you Father! I love You! Amen

Uncertainties

Dear Lord,

The future for me is so obscure. I have no idea where my life is headed. All I know is where I have been today and I thank You for leading me through this day. Lord, will I ever get married? Will I find the perfect job? Will I ever own my own home? Where can I fit in at my church? Lord, there are so many questions that only You know the answers to. Father, as I end this day I give them to You and ask that You do as You see fit. I am at Your mercy always, loving Father. Thank You for this day and I pray that if tomorrow comes that answers may come with it. I love You! Amen

Salt And Light

Glorious One,

Today was a wonderful day! Thank you for allowing me to be your vessel in spreading Your love to others through my actions today. I was the salt and the light to many people today. I know there will always be nay sayers but there are also lost people on very fertile soil. Lord, I pray that the seeds I planted today were on fertile soil. I pray, Lord, that you will water these seeds and reap a bountiful harvest. Thank you for this day! I love You! Amen

Rough Day

Lord above,

Today was a rough one. I am late on paying bills. I need new tires on my car and that caused me to almost have an accident. I feel like I am in a dead-end job. My spouse and kids are driving me crazy! Life is out of control right now, Father! Lord, I need Your stability right now. You are my Rock! Refresh my Spirit with song! Refresh my mind with Your Word! Refresh my soul within this prayer, Lord! I am at Your mercy and I know You are with me always. I pray, Lord, that You make my paths straight and iron out all of these trials. What can I learn from these trials? I place these all in Your hands. I love You, Father! Amen

Prayer for Anxiety and stress

Heavenly Father, When I feel crushed by my own worries, Lift my mind and help me to see the truth. When fear grips me tight and I feel I cannot move, Free my heart and help me to take things one step at a time. When I can't express the turmoil inside, Calm me with Your quiet words of love. I choose to trust in You, each day, each hour, each moment of my life. I know deep down that I can cast these cares on You, that you have taken these anxious thoughts and by dying on the cross, You have set me free. I choose to trust in You, each day, each hour, each moment of my life. I know deep down that I live in Your grace, forgiven, restored by Your sacrifice, You have set me free. Amen.

Prayer for self-confidence

(a prayer for courage, strength and confidence in myself)

Oh Father,

Thank you Lord that I am a daughter (son) of a king loved and cherished, and my inheritance is eternal goodness.

So today I wear my crown like a princess (prince). Full of humility, for I do not earn this honour, I simply choose to live in it. I place this prize upon my head, a jewel already paid for, this symbol of belonging. I feel the grace of God within my heart, grace that enables me to try hard and not to fear failure. Grace that calls me to stay true to my values and visions, but not to be overwhelmed by them. Grace to walk tall, following in your footsteps.

Thank you Lord, for I am daughter (son) of the king, a princess/prince with a crown of jewels, and a child with a loving heavenly Father.

Amen.

Praises

Oh Lord,

You led me safely through this day! May Your Name be praised always! Lord, I praise You for so many things! I praise You for my family, job, car, house, friends, church, Bible, prayer time, and most importantly, Jesus! Lord, thank You for Jesus! He bled and died for me! He loved me enough to embrace those nail-scarred hands and feet! Oh, how He loves me! I praise Your Name and the Name of Jesus Christ! I love You! Amen

Strength

Father,

I am weak right now. There is so much going on in my life physically and emotionally that I am at my breaking point! I need Your strength to make it through these times. Father, I pray that tonight while I sleep You will refresh my mind and strength for tomorrow morning. Lord, I pray that You will watch over me as I sleep and bring pleasant thoughts into my mind as I dream away. Thank You for loving me, Lord! Amen

Anticipation

Father,

Here I am ready to fall asleep and I can't help but think about what Heaven will be like. I imagine beautiful walkways where the saints talk and sing praises to You! I imagine the room that Jesus has prepared for me! A room prepared by the greatest designer ever! I imagine talking with the people that I love right now and the ones that are already with You! I can't wait to see the 12 gates surrounding it! I can't wait to experience Jesus for the first time there! Oh Father, I will be in Your presence! In the presence of Yahweh! You are the biggest reward of all-time! Thank You for loving me so much, Father! Amen

Inspirational prayer

Lord, You are my pillar of strength and shield. You are also my Shepherd — the One who always guides me. Father, as I/we head out for the day today, be with us, and guide our thoughts and actions. With Your help, good and new things will happen to us and any environment we might be. Thank You for listening to me Lord, Amen.

Prayer for wisdom

Dear God, please give me the wisdom to operate in the right. Any situation that I find myself in, I want You to give me the wisdom to make the best of my options and decisions. Protect from mistakes that'll hamper any plan that You have for me. Thank You God Almighty. Amen.

Prayer for hope

Father, I have faced many challenges all my life. Some with impossible odds, and others that were simply unbelievable. But still, throughout both of them, You came through for me.

Father in Heaven, I stand before You today because I hope for a better future. I pray that my investments, plans, and relationships will come to fruition. Walking in Your light has thought me perseverance and by Your power, I will persevere and win. Thank You for this session, and You deserve nothing less than eternal glory Lord. In Jesus Name I pray.

Prayer for faith and trust

My Father in Heaven, this is not the 1st time I'll be before You and certainly not the last. I pray for faith and trust in You and Your words Lord above. Do not let my faith waver, because perseverance is a value of my worth. As for my trust, give me insight into Your words, so that I may consume and use them. I thank You for standing with me always. Amen.

Short prayer for guidance

Dear Lord,

I can not see the way ahead and at the moment I feel so confused.
So today I ask that your hand would be upon mine.
Please lead me safely through.
Guide my heart, my mind and body to navigate the way.

I put my trust in you.

Amen.

Short prayer for strength

Dear Father God,

I know that when I am weak you are my strength. You understand that these are the times when I need to be carried by you. I pray that you would gently renew my strength, speak your words of encouragement into my mind, sing songs of hope over my soul and awaken my heart.

I look to you.

Amen.

Short prayer for peace

Dear Lord,

Your peace surpasses all understanding.
Like a moment of stillness within a storm,
Like a place of quiet within a crowd,
Or a soft area to rest on a hard journey.
Help me to know your peace in my heart.

Amen.

Short prayer for protection

Dear Lord,

You have placed a helmet of salvation on my head -
that I might have peace of mind.
You have placed a breastplate of righteousness upon my chest -
so that my heart may be protected and safe.
You have placed a shield of faith in my hand -
so that as I journey no evil can stand against me.
You have placed the sword of the spirit in my hand -
that I may release those in need.

You are with me.
Thank you.

Amen.

Prayer for safety and protection

May the three enfold you
Father, Son and Holy Spirit
Hold you safe and hold you strong

May the three encompass you
Father, Son and Holy Spirit
Encircle your life each day and night

May the three protect you
Father, Son and Holy Spirit
Guard your door and keep each gate

May the three watch over you
Father, Son and Holy Spirit
Still your heart and calm all fear

Wedding prayer

Ground and source of all life, we stop and recall with gratitude the gift of life. We are grateful for the love of [name] and [name] parents, who raised them from childhood with care and concern, bringing them to this day. We are grateful for the example of [name] and [name] love in their new commitment to one another. We express our gratitude to those who grew and harvested the food we will share today, those who prepared it and those who will serve it. We are grateful also to the wind and the rain, the sun and the earth, who provide not only this meal but all of our life on this planet. Let us take a moment of silence now in gratitude for life. [10 second pause] Amen.

Another wedding prayer

Heavenly Father, we thank you for your love, which we have seen today reflected in [name] and [name]'s eyes. We have come from many places, many backgrounds, many beliefs, but [name] and [name] have drawn us together to share this meal together, their first meal as a married couple. We are grateful for love which seeks us and finds us. We are grateful for this meal. We pray your blessing upon those who prepared it and those who will serve it. We ask that you bless Jane and John and us as we celebrate tonight. We pray in the name of Jesus Christ. Amen.

A Prayer to Recharge

Dear Lord, You have brought me to the beginning of a new day. As the world is renewed fresh and clean, so I ask You to renew my heart with Your strength and purpose. Forgive me the errors of yesterday and bless me to walk closer in Your way today. This is the day I begin my life anew; shine through me so that every person I meet may feel Your presence in me. Take my hand, precious Lord for I cannot make it by myself. Amen.

A Prayer For My Career

Dear God, I thank you for my job. You have provided me with steady income and I'm so thankful. I pray that You watch over me today at work and I pray that there are no accidents, so that everyone can go back to their homes. I thank you that my job has provided an income to support me and my family. I thank you for the provisions that You have given me. I pray for safe travels to and from work and I pray that You will use me as You see fit today for Your glory. Amen.

A Prayer For Opportunity

Dear Lord, I pray today that I will yield my spirit completely to You, that You may use me as You please. I pray that You will provide me opportunities to show people how much You mean to me. Give me discretion to know what to say and how to say it. Make me bold enough that I may proclaim salvation cheerfully and joyfully. I pray that the seeds You allow me to plant will grow and mature. I am forever grateful for the cross; may I proclaim it in a contagious way today. Amen.

A Prayer For Contentment

Dear God, I pray that I will stay focused on You today. I pray that You will constantly remind me to be content in all of my circumstances. I pray that You will fill me up that I may be joyful all day, even if stress creeps in. I know that through my contentment, You will be glorified. I want to honor You, Father, in all that I do.

Amen.

A Prayer for our Prayer Life

Father, we praise you for your ever-permeating presence, and your omnipotence over our lives. You have been where we are going, and because you know what lies ahead, you now what's best for us. God, You have surrounded us with so much at which to marvel. The winter snow and Christmas lights, the sounds of carols and excited kids. Thank you for blessing us in abundance, and forgive for rushing past all of the good that you bring to our daily path. Fill our hearts with reminders to stop and pray this Christmas season. As we hustle and stress, let your Holy Spirit help us to remember you and recall your promise to love us always. In Jesus' Name, Amen.

A Prayer for Our Homes

Father, we praise you for protecting us and providing for us. We are able to sleep in warm bed and close our door to the cold, while others dream of shelter and safety that a home provides. We thank you for our home, and pray that you bless it and keep it safe from fire, flood, wind, and intruders. May it be a place that reflects your grace. Bless those who are homeless. Come to their aid, Lord. Protect them and keep them safe while they are exposed to the elements, and may their heads find a warm place to rest this holiday season. In Jesus' Name, Amen.

A Prayer for Financial Provision

Father, we praise you for providing for us. We know that you give us what we need, and that it doesn't always come in the form of dollar signs. Father, help us to see Christ first above all else this Christmas. Help us to put the lists down and pick up your Word. Guide our giving towards others that need to experience the love of Christ-inspired generosity. Help us to give gifts out of the love we have for you and each other, not out of requirement or competition. Bless those who have nothing to give this Christmas, and who are suffering financially. Comfort them, and uphold them. In Jesus' Name, Amen.

A Prayer for Safety while travelling

Father, we praise you for travel, and holiday reunions. You are not surprised by the weather or the delays in our travel. The world rests in your hands that created and sustain it. We confess our tendency to worry about whether we will make it to where we are going, and worry about relative and friends that we are expectantly awaiting the arrival of. Just as sure as Jesus came to earth when you said it was time, our lives will run according to your plan. Help us to remember the gospel truth not to worry, and increase our trust in you as we travel. Protect us as we go to and fro, and layer us in blankets of security as we pass through bad whether and harrowing road conditions, flight delays and emergencies. Bless us and protect us, Lord. In Jesus' Name, Amen.

A Prayer for Health

Father, we praise you for the human body, and all of it's amazing capabilities. Though we can accomplish great things, our frailty is a stark reality. For those that lie in hospitals and hospice care this Christmas, we pray a special blessing over their ailments. Heal them, Lord, in your will and your way. Comfort them when they are lonely, and encourage them when the pain threatens to steal their sanity. Be with them in a special way this Christmas. Thank you for our good health. Sustain us and heal us, Jesus, with your authoritative hand over humanity. In Jesus' Name, Amen.

A Prayer for Our Kids

Father, we praise you for the innocent hearts of children. May they be filled with the excitement and glory of Christmas. Let them hear your voice over all others, especially our patience stricken sharpness. Forgive us for snapping on their tiny Christmas spirits, in our impatience to get our lists checked twice. Help us to enjoy the magic of Christmas with our children, so that they will pass it down to the next generation. Though there are many fun holiday traditions, let Christ reign over them all. Let them know He is the reason for the season, and let them come to Him with their hearts surrendered. Bless parents to be a flashlight for their kids this Christmas, lighting the way to Jesus' feet for them. In Jesus' Name, Amen.

A Prayer to Stretch Time

Father, we praise you for time. Your creation amazes us. You know how long to make each day, week, month, and year. Nothing eludes you. You're creations and your plan are perfect. Forgive us for blocking off our days into controlled increments, when you are the one who holds the key to our time. Bless our minutes, especially this Christmas. Help us to release our grip on how we think the days should be, and let you intervene with your sovereign hand by lifting our minutes up to you in prayer. Stretch them when we are rushing haphazardly, and slow them when we need a moment to marinate. Let all of the time we spend celebrating Christmas, reflect Christ. In Jesus' Name, Amen.

A Prayer for Christmas

Father, we praise You for Christmas. Thank you for leaving us your Word. Teach us to treasure it, and through the power of the Holy Spirit that lives in us, reveal more of your character to us each time we turn over a new page. Show us our purpose in this life as we seek you each day in Scripture. Thank you for sending your Son to earth to save us. He is the Word. Born to Mary in a stable, a vulnerable baby boy, He walked the earth that we trod. God, Himself, among us. Emmanuel. Bless our hearts to be filled with the awe and wonder that surrounded the shepherds as the angles sang of Jesus' birth. Help us to know you a little better than we did before this Christmas. Through the stories and the lessons in the Bible, you reach out to us, to teach us who we are. Praise you for loving us so personally and perfectly. Thank you, Jesus, for coming to save us and promising never to leave us. In Jesus' Name, Amen.

Dedication of the Day

Father, I dedicate this new day to you;

as I go about my work.

I ask you to bless those with whom I come in contact.

Lord, I pray for all men and women

who work to earn their living;

give them satisfaction in what they do.

Spirit of God,

comfort the unemployed and their families;

they are your children and my brothers and sisters.

I ask you to help them find work soon.

Amen.

By St. Ignatius Loyola

Afternoon Prayer

Most glorious God,
As I pause in the midst of this day,
I invite You into this moment of prayer.

I ask Your pardon for any way that I have failed to love today.
For my pride, envy, gluttony, greed, lust, sloth and anger,
I beg for Your forgiveness.

Once again, I dedicate this day to You.
I pray for humility, kindness, temperance, charity, chastity, diligence and patience.

Help me, Lord, to listen to Your gentle voice
And to trust in Your guidance and grace.

My life is Yours, dear Lord.
My life is Yours.

May I hold nothing back from You.
May I fulfill my duties this day in accord with Your perfect will.

I love You, dear Lord.
I love You with all my heart.
Help me to love You and others with all my might.
Amen.

Prayer at Night

My precious Lord,
As this day comes to a close,
I take this moment to turn to You.
Help me, in this moment of quiet, to examine my day.

(Do a brief examination of conscience or review the examination below)

Lord, I thank You for helping me to see my sin.
Please give to me the grace of humility
So that I can admit all my sin without reserve.

I pray that every sin will be forgiven,
And I open myself to Your grace
So that Your merciful Heart will create me anew.

I also call to mind the way in which You were present to me this day.

(Take a moment to ponder the graces God blessed you with this day)

Lord, I thank You for the blessings of this day.
Please help me to see these blessings as Your divine presence in my life.

May I turn from sin and turn to You.
Your presence in my life brings great joy;

My sin leads to sorrow and despair.

I choose You as my Lord.
I choose You as my guide
And pray for Your abundant blessings tomorrow.

May this night be restful in You.
May it be a night of renewal.

Speak to me, Lord, as I sleep.
Guard me and protect me the whole night through.

My guardian angel, Saint Joseph, my Blessed Mother,
Intercede for me now and always.

Amen.

SURRENDER, HEALING & FORGIVENESS PRAYERS

Prayer of Abandonment

Father,

I abandon myself into your hands;

do with me what you will.

Whatever you may do, I thank you:

I am ready for all, I accept all.

Let only your will be done in me,

and in all your creatures –

I wish no more than this, O Lord.

Into your hands I commend my soul:

I offer it to you with all the love of my heart,

for I love you, Lord, and so need to give myself,

to surrender myself into your hands without reserve,

and with boundless confidence,

for you are my Father.

Amen.

Charles de Foucauld

Prayer of Surrender

Take, Lord, and receive all my liberty,
My memory, my understanding
And my entire will,
All I have and call my own.

You have given all to me.
To you, Lord, I return it.

Everything is yours; do with it what you will.
Give me only your love and your grace.
That is enough for me.

Amen.

Prayer of St. Ignatius of Loyola

Pleading for Mercy and Forgiveness of Sin

From Psalm 51

O loving and gracious God, have mercy.
Have pity upon me and take away the awful stain of my sin.
Oh, wash me, cleanse me from this guilt. Let me be pure again.
For I admit my shameful deed-it haunts me day and night.
It is a sin against You and Your infinite mercy.

Create in me a new, clean heart, O God.
Purify me and make me white as snow.
Cleanse my thoughts and desires.
Restore to me again the joy of your salvation, and make me willing to obey you.

Jesus, have mercy on me.
Jesus, have mercy on me.
Jesus, have mercy on me.

Jesus, I trust in You.
Jesus, I trust in You.
Jesus, I trust in You.

Amen.

Help with Depression

O Christ Jesus,

when all is darkness
and I feel my weakness and helplessness,
give me a sense of Your presence,
Your love, and Your strength.
Help me to have perfect trust
in Your protecting love
and strengthening power,
so that nothing may frighten or worry me,
for, living close to You,
I shall see Your hand,
Your purpose, Your will through all things.

Amen.

By Saint Ignatius of Loyola

Overcoming Sinful Passions

Dear Jesus, in the Sacrament of the Altar,

be forever thanked and praised.

Love, worthy of all celestial and terrestrial love!

Who, out of infinite love for me,

ungrateful sinner,

didst assume our human nature,

didst shed Thy most Precious Blood in the cruel scourging,

and didst expire on a shameful Cross for our eternal welfare!

Now illumined with lively faith,

with the outpouring of my whole soul and the fervor of my heart,

I humbly beseech Thee,

through the infinite merits of Thy painful sufferings,

give me strength and courage to destroy every evil passion which sways my heart,

to bless Thee by the exact fulfillment of my duties,

supremely to hate all sin,

and thus to become a Saint.

Amen.

Prayer Before the Crucifix

Look down upon me, good and gentle Jesus
while before Your face I humbly kneel and,
with burning soul,
pray and beseech You
to fix deep in my heart lively sentiments
of faith, hope, and charity;
true contrition for my sins,
and a firm purpose of amendment.

While I contemplate,
with great love and tender pity,
Your five most precious wounds,
pondering over them within me
and calling to mind the words which David,
Your prophet, said to You, my Jesus:

"They have pierced My hands and My feet,
they have numbered all My bones."

Amen.

COMMON CATHOLIC PRAYERS

Apostles Creed

I believe in God,
the Father almighty,
Creator of heaven and earth,
and in Jesus Christ, his only Son, our Lord,
who was conceived by the Holy Spirit,
born of the Virgin Mary,
suffered under Pontius Pilate,
was crucified, died and was buried;
he descended into hell;
on the third day he rose again from the dead;
he ascended into heaven,
and is seated at the right hand of God the Father almighty;
from there he will come to judge the living and the dead.

I believe in the Holy Spirit,
the holy catholic Church,
the communion of saints,
the forgiveness of sins,
the resurrection of the body,
and life everlasting. Amen.

Our Father

Our Father, who art in heaven, hallowed be thy name. Thy kingdom come, thy will be done, on earth, as it is in heaven. Give us this day our daily bread and forgive us our trespasses as we forgive those who trespass against us; and lead us not into temptation, but deliver us from evil. Amen.

Hail Mary

Hail Mary, full of grace,
the Lord is with you.
Blessed are you among women,
and blessed is the fruit of your womb, Jesus.
Holy Mary, Mother of God,
pray for us sinners,
now and at the hour of our death.
Amen.

Glory Be

Glory be to the Father,
and to the Son,
and to the Holy Spirit.
As it was in the beginning,
is now, and ever shall be,
world without end.
Amen.

Nicene Creed

I believe in one God,
the Father almighty,
maker of heaven and earth,
of all things visible and invisible.

I believe in one Lord Jesus Christ,
the Only Begotten Son of God,
born of the Father before all ages.
God from God, Light from Light,
true God from true God,
begotten, not made, consubstantial with the Father;
through him all things were made.
For us men and for our salvation
he came down from heaven,

and by the Holy Spirit was incarnate of the Virgin Mary,
and became man.

For our sake he was crucified under Pontius Pilate,
he suffered death and was buried,
and rose again on the third day
in accordance with the Scriptures.
He ascended into heaven
and is seated at the right hand of the Father.
He will come again in glory
to judge the living and the dead

and his kingdom will have no end.

I believe in the Holy Spirit, the Lord, the giver of life,
who proceeds from the Father and the Son,
who with the Father and the Son is adored and glorified,
who has spoken through the prophets.

I believe in one, holy, catholic and apostolic Church.
I confess one Baptism for the forgiveness of sins
and I look forward to the resurrection of the dead
and the life of the world to come. Amen.

Prayer Before Meals

Bless us, O Lord, and these your gifts which we are about to receive from your goodness.
Through Christ our Lord.
Amen.

Act of Contrition

O my God, I am heartily sorry for having offended You, and I detest all my sins because of Your just punishments, but most of all because they offend You, my God, who are all-good and deserving of all my love. I firmly resolve, with the help of Your grace, to sin no more and to avoid the near occasion of sin. Amen.

PRAYERS FOR EVERY DAY OF THE WEEK

Sunday

Lord, I love you because you hear my voice and my supplications (Psalm 116:1). I have confidence that when I ask anything according to your will, you hear me (1 John 5:14). Thank you for hearing me.

Lord, please forgive me for my sins. They are many. Forgive me for the idols in my life that I put before you and for the times that I try to be my own god. Change my heart, Lord. Make me pure and righteous in your sight and by the power of your blood that you shed for me. Thank you for your promise of forgiveness.

Lord, today I pray for my leaders and other leaders all over our country and world. I pray for the pastors, elders, deacons, and Bible teachers at my church and other churches. Please bind the enemy from attacking them. Keep them safe under your wing of protection. Amen.

Monday

Heavenly Father, you are sovereign, and you are my hope. You have always been my confidence, and you are my confidence today (Psalm 71:5). In my suffering, you comfort me (2 Corinthians 1:5). Thank you for being the one who I can always count on.

Today, please have mercy on me. Allow your grace to rain down on me because I am sinful. Please forgive me, Lord. Forgive me for taking my life for granted and for my ungratefulness for all you've given me. Forgive me for any entitlement I display in my heart or mind.

Today I pray for missionaries all over the world. Please provide for all of their needs—spiritual, physical, and emotional—and strengthen them. Give them the words they need to bring others to you and give them a heart of service so that others may see your love through their actions. Protect them from the enemies' schemes and from other people who seek to harm them. Amen.

Tuesday

Lord, your mercies are new every morning because of your great love for me. I know the enemy will never consume me (Lamentations 3:22-23). I praise you, Lord, for your faithfulness! Thank you for your love!

Today, please forgive me for all impatience and lack of self-control I display in my life. Forgive me for demanding my own way and not loving other people by bearing with them and showing them grace. Change me, Lord. Make me loving in this way.

Today, I pray for people who are homeless or poor. I pray for people who do not have what they need to live healthy and secure lives. Please have mercy on them, Lord. Please strengthen them and provide for them in ways that only you can.

More than anything, please use their circumstances to bring them to you. Also, please open my eyes to the needs around me. Help me to see people in these situations as your beloved children. Give me compassion for them. Forgive me when I judge them. Show me how I can help and equip me to do so. Amen.

Wednesday

Heavenly Father, you are my salvation. You are who sustains me and gives me life. You are my strength, my defense, and I do not need to be afraid. Whatever happens in my life, I know you are there protecting me (Isaiah 12:2). Thank you for your protection, Lord.

Lord, today forgive me for my thoughts that do not honor you. Forgive me for thinking thoughts of jealousy, slander, and malice. Please help me to think on things that are true, noble, right, pure, lovely, admirable, excellent, and praiseworthy (Philippians 4:8). Thank you for giving me the ability through the power of the Holy Spirit to renew my mind (Romans 12:2).

Today, Lord, I pray for people who are sick. I pray for people with all kinds of illnesses—physical and psychological. I pray for people who are in the hospital, homebound, chronically sick, and disabled. I pray for people with cancer and other life-threatening diseases. I pray for those who will not get better or recover in their lifetime. Please comfort them and their family members and bring all of them to salvation through their experience. Amen.

Thursday

Lord, you are just in all your ways (Deuteronomy 32:4). In all ways you are righteous, and I praise you (Revelation 15:3). You exercise justice toward all of humanity (Genesis 18:25). Thank you for being a God of justice and mercy.

Today, Lord, forgive me for the sinful things I say. Forgive me for gossiping, slandering, criticizing, exaggerating, and lying, even if slightly. Please help my "...conversation be always full of grace, seasoned with salt, so that [I] may know how to answer everyone" (Colossians 4:6).

Lord, today I lift up people who are oppressed. This includes people who do not have basic human rights, people involved in human trafficking and slavery, people who are being persecuted, women and children who are abused and not cared for, orphans, widows, and unborn babies who face abortion. Please have mercy on them and do miracles to save them from their torment. Most of all, draw them to you so that you receive all the glory. Amen.

Friday

Lord, you are the way, the truth and the life (John 14:6). Your Word gives me life and sustains me (John 8:32). I honor you for the hope of eternal life you offer me and the life you give me now. Thank you, Lord, for giving me life.

Today I ask you to forgive me for any resentment and anger in my heart. Please forgive me for not forgiving other people. I know your Word says, "For if you forgive other people when they sin against you, your heavenly Father will also forgive you. But if you do not forgive others their sins, your Father will not forgive your sins" (Matthew 6:14-15). I need forgiveness from you, Lord; so please, help me to forgive.

I pray for my friends and family today. I pray that you meet each of their individual needs. Keep them healthy in all ways. I pray that you will heal any discord between me and my friends and family and any discord that is between them.

I also pray for each of their salvation. If any of my friends and family have not given their life to you, or are not following you wholeheartedly, please, Lord, lead them to you through the power of the Holy Spirit. Amen.

Saturday

Lord, "there is no one holy like [you are]; there is no one besides you; there is no rock like [you]" (1 Samuel 2:2). You, Lord, deserve constant honor (Revelation 4:8). As I end the week, I look to you as the only one who deserves my praise. Thank you for being my rock and my salvation.

Lord, please forgive me for the ways that I neglect time with you. Forgive me for allowing busyness to take over so that I'm not spending adequate time in your Word and in prayer. Lord, give me a heart for you and only you! When I get complacent in my spiritual growth, prick my soul and bring me back to you.

Today I pray for unbelievers in my community and all over the world. I ask the Holy Spirit to come into their lives and save their souls so that they, too, can have a relationship with you now and eternal life with you in heaven. Please, Lord, allow every person on this earth to hear your name and accept your gift. Then, please come back quickly. Amen.

PRAYERS FOR EVENING AND NIGHT

For the Night

O Lord, I pray for your support all the day long, until the shadows lengthen and the evening comes, and the busy world is hushed, and the fever of life is over, and my work is done. Then in your mercy, grant me and my family a safe lodging, and a holy rest, and peace at the last.

Amen.

O God, who is the life of mortal men, the light of the faithful, the strength of those who labor, and the repose of the dead; I thank you for the timely blessings of the day, and humbly beg for your merciful protection all this night. Bring me and my loved ones, I beseech you, in safety to the morning hours; through him who died for us and rose again, your Son, our Jesus Christ.

Amen.

A Short Evening Prayer Devotion

Our Father, who art in heaven, Hallowed be thy Name. Thy kingdom come. Thy will be done, On earth as it is in heaven. Give us this day our daily bread. And forgive us our trespasses, As we forgive those who trespass against us. And lead us not into temptation, But deliver us from evil. For thine is the kingdom, and the power, and the glory, for ever and ever.

Amen.

A Short Evening Prayer Devotion 2

Lighten our darkness, we beseech thee, O Lord; and by thy great mercy defend us from all perils and dangers of this night; for the love of thy only Son, our Savior, Jesus Christ.

Amen.

Prayer of a Weary Apostle

Thanks I give to you, my God, for the day that is ending, and thanks for the coming night. Bring sleep to the weary, bring repose to those I love, and give me rest until tomorrow. Be present, O Lord, and protect your children through the silent hours of this night, that we who are wearied with the work and changes of this fleeting world, may rest upon your eternal changelessness.

In this day that is ending I have not been all that I should have been. Help me, my God, to be less harsh towards others, more gentle, more patient. Make me too, more determined, more demanding of myself, more truthful in speaking, more faithful in my promises, more active in my work, more obedient and more submissive to your will; let me be cheerful, too, and may tomorrow be a finer, fuller day than this.

Amen.

Prayer at the End of Day

Jesus Christ, my God, I adore You and thank you for all the graces You have given me this day. I offer You my sleep and all the moments of this night, and I beg of you to keep me without sin. Therefore, I put myself within your sacred care and under the mantle of your Holy Spirit. Let Your holy angels stand about me and keep me in peace; and let your blessing be upon me.

Amen.

Prayer for a Day Lived

Lord, You have always given bread for the coming day; and though I am poor, today I believe.

Lord, You have always given strength for the coming day; and though I am weak, today I believe.

Lord, You have always given peace for the coming day; and though of anxious heart, today I believe.

Lord, You have always kept me safe in trials; and now, tried as I am, today I believe.

Lord, You have always marked he road for the coming day; and though it may be hidden, today I believe.

Lord, You have always lightened this darkness of mine; and though the night is here, today I believe.

Lord, You have always spoken when time was ripe; and though you be silent now, today I believe.

Amen.

Prayer at the End of the Day 2

My Lord, I thank you for having given me life, and for having made me to know, love, and serve you all the days of my life and for eternity. I thank you for my faith and for the work and pleasure in the day that I am completing. I beg your pardon for my offenses and omissions of the day, and resolve to make tomorrow a better day. Be with me as I live out the rest of my day. May I do so in your holy grace and good favor.

Amen

Prayer for the night coming

Heavenly Father, to your goodness I commend myself this night, humbly asking for your protection through its darkness and dangers. I am helpless and dependent; graciously preserve me. For all whom I love and value, for every friend and connection, I equally pray; however divided and far asunder, I know that we are alike before you, and under your eye. May we be equally united in faith and fear, in fervent devotion towards you, and in your merciful protection this night. Pardon oh Lord! the imperfections of these my prayers, and accept them through the mediation of our blessed savior, Jesus Christ.

Amen.

A Bedtime Prayer

Give me light in the season of night, I beseech you, O Lord, and grant that my rest may be without sin, and my waking to your service; that I may come in peace and safety to the waking of the great day; through Jesus Christ our Lord. Amen.

Amen.

Prayer for God's Protection through this Night.

I beseech you to continue your gracious protection to me and my family this night. Defend us from all dangers, and from the fear of them; that we may enjoy such refreshing sleep as may fit us for the duties of the coming day. And grant me grace always to live in such a state that I may never be afraid to die; so that, living and dying, I may be yours, through the merits and satisfaction of your Son Christ Jesus, in whose name I offer up these my imperfect prayers.

Amen.

PRAYERS FOR FAMILY

A Prayer for my Husband

(a morning prayer)

Lord I thank you for my husband, For the comfort of walking hand in hand with him. Lord I thank you for his faithfulness. May you always guide his footsteps to love and follow you. I thank you for his patience. May you be his strength, root his life in goodness and grace. I thank you for his provision. May his work be blessed, bearing the fruit of security and hope. I thank you for his wisdom. May you protect him and guide his heart and mind. And I thank you for our friendship. As we draw near to You may we feel closer than ever before. In tears, in laughter, in all that we do, May we remember the joy The inexpressible comfort Of being joined through our marriage to You.

A morning prayer for my wife

(a short daily prayer for her protection, health and well-being)

Father, Watch over my beloved wife Keep her safe Sing songs of love to her soul Fill her heart Renew her with health and strength Hold her steady Inspire her mind with hope Guide her footsteps Bless her day with happiness and laughter Thank you for her Amen

Prayer for brother

Heavenly Father, please bless my brother. My brother was born premature (born in 7th month) . He had learning disabilities. Was termed as a slow learner. Somehow he completed his X and XII and did few small courses and got a job. We found him a good girl and by God's grace got him married too. But in a year his wife left him and now they stay separate. He has lost his job and is with my parents. Requesting prayers to help him find a job, prayers for his wife's return, and for his happiness

Prayer for my sister

Dear heavenly Father,

I come to you today completely trusting in your goodness and mercy. I appeal to your loving Spirit to watch over my sister. I praise you for her life and her soul. Thank you for her presence in my life.

Look upon my sister with your tenderness and grace. If she hurts – bring her healing. If she's afraid – give her courage. If she has fallen – lift her up in forgiveness.

And most of all dear Lord, let her know she is loved. Let her know I love her. Let her know you love her. And let love heal even her deepest wounds.

Give her confidence knowing she is your child. Oh heavenly Father, embrace my sister's heart. Bless her my Lord. Let her be healthy, free and protected in the strength of your loving arms.

In Jesus name,

Amen.

Prayer For Daughter's Health

Loving Lord, I praise You that we are fearfully and wonderfully made and that You are the one Whose healing touch is still as powerful today as it was in the times of Abraham, Isaac, and Jacob, and so I come to ask for that same healing power to be poured out over my daughter, who is not at all well.

Lord, You know the exact reason why she is so poorly.. for You formed her in the womb and scheduled each day of her life.. and so I ask that You in Your grace and goodness You would minister to her need, and heal her speedily.

Lord, I feel so helpless as I stand by and watch the progression of this illness, with little knowledge of what I really ought to do, and so I come to You to plead You healing power over her, and ask that You touch every part of her body and flow through her in each area that needs Your loving touch and healing hand.

I pray that her body may be quickly healed, and restored to life and health.. and I will not forget to give You all the praise and glory – for You are God who hears and answers prayer – in Jesus name I pray,

Amen

A prayer for my son

Father in heaven, Help me to be a good parent. As I dwell in your love, may I give my own son an ocean of love to abide in. As I receive your forgiveness, may I always be ready to forgive my own dear son and offer him a new day. As I hope in you, and look forward to the future knowing your guidance. May I gently protect and lead my own beloved son into a place of hope and vision for his future. Lord, help me to be a good parent. Amen.

A prayer for married couples

O Lord, You are Lord over all creation. Everyday we are surrounded by the miracle of life. Your creativity bursts across the skies at sunset, it emerges from spring buds that bloom. Thank you for the beauty of marriage. Like three streams that merge into one single river, you are journeying with us. You are the creative, restoring current that runs through our relationship. May we stand strong in our friendship like a tall oak tree. May we pull together through the different seasons of our lives so that we become closer. May we ride out the storms and rest in the fair weather. May we care for one another, so that we blossom and bloom as individuals. May we have your vision as we soar above the everyday to glimpse the kingdom of heaven. May we learn the truth of real beauty as we change and age together. And may we reflect your love, hope, and truth that you have poured into our union. Thank you that through your strength and grace we are able to love, care and provide for our loved ones and the wider world. Amen.

Praying For Your Children

Father, I come to you in the beautiful name of Jesus
The name that is above all things

Oh Lord, I pray for everyone in the life of my children,
be it family, friends or teachers.

I pray that you would raise up and birth spiritual heroes for them
People that they can look up to
That have integrity with a positive energy
That are living right lives

Lord, help my children to make the right friends
Let them choose godly friends that are walking with you
Friends that are smart, sober-minded and of good behavior
Friends that will have a meaningful impact in their life

Knowing that through you Oh God
all things are possible
I pray, Amen!

Prayer For Your Children 2

Dear Lord
Today I come to you in faith
knowing that through you all things are possible

I present my children before you and I ask you to guide them
Help them make good decisions
that will have a positive impact on their future
Equip them for the plans you have in store for them
Help them understand the necessity of
making time for you in prayer
Let them hear your instructive voice
and the teaching of the wise people in their lives

Give them peace of mind and boost their confidence
while walking in this world
I pray that they would find their place in life and in society
And not wander and waste the years of their life

Help them among their friends to boldly stand up for You
being an example in words, in behavior, in love, in attitude,
in faith, and in purity

Lord, help my children to be good stewards of their abilities
And become the person you want them to be.

In the Holy name of Jesus
I pray, Amen!

Prayer for loved ones

I pray for my family and loved ones that You, God Almighty safeguard us. Do not leave our side Father, and please, make provisions for all of our needs. We shall not want because You'll always be guiding on our actions and protecting us. I thank You for the answered prayers Oh Lord, And In Jesus Name I pray.

A Prayer For Family

Dear God, thank you for the gift of family and friends. Holding them in my heart is one of the most precious things I can never get tired of. Bless everyone, for they deserve all goodness You have given to me. If I may do something wrong today, please forgive me. Amen.

A Prayer for Parents

Father, we praise you for parenthood. Though the hours are long and the worry is overwhelming, we know that you placed our children with us purposefully. Thank you for equipping us to raise them and guide them to you, and forgive us for taking sole possession of their lives as we cling to them in love. Guides us, as we guide them, this Christmas. Help us to steer around the commercialism of the season to reflect upon your Son, Jesus. Father, we pray that we represent your love as their parents the best we humanly can. Bless and fill our hearts with patience this holiday season. In Jesus' Name, Amen.

A Prayer for Family Gatherings

Father, we praise you for our families. We pray for those who do not have anyone to share the holiday season with. Will you make them evident to us, and stir our hearts to include them in our celebration this Christmas. Help us to be the reach of your arm to love someone who is experiencing the pain of loneliness this year. Bless our family gatherings to be peaceful and Christ-centered. Bless our lives to reflect your light, especially to those who do not believe in you yet. Help us to reflect on our own hearts, and reveal anyone we need to forgive, without waiting for an apology. Bless us to forgive as you forgave, and embrace the gift that is our family this Christmas …and always. In Jesus' Name, Amen.

All information for the book was collected from open sources.

Printed in Great Britain
by Amazon